STUDY GUIDE

The Pigman
Paul Zindel

WITH CONNECTIONS

HOLT, RINEHART AND WINSTON
Harcourt Brace & Company

Austin • New York • Orlando • Atlanta • San Francisco • Boston • Dallas • Toronto • London

Staff Credits

Associate Director: Mescal Evler

Manager of Editorial Operations: Robert R. Hoyt

Managing Editor: Bill Wahlgren

Executive Editor: Emily Shenk

Component Editor: Mikki Gibson

Editorial Staff: *Assistant Managing Editor,* Mandy Beard; *Copyediting Supervisor,* Michael Neibergall; *Senior Copyeditor,* Mary Malone; *Copyeditors,* Joel Bourgeois, Jon Hall, Jeffrey T. Holt, Jane M. Kominek, Susan Sandoval; *Editorial Coordinators,* Marie H. Price, Jill Chertudi, Mark Holland, Marcus Johnson, Tracy DeMont; *Support Staff,* Pat Stover, Matthew Villalobos; *Word Processors,* Ruth Hooker, Margaret Sanchez, Kelly Keeley

Permissions: Carrie Jones, Catherine Paré

Design: *Art Director, Book & Media Design,* Joe Melomo

Image Services: *Art Buyer, Supervisor,* Elaine Tate

Prepress Production: Beth Prevelige, Sergio Durante

Manufacturing Coordinator: Michael Roche

Development Coordinator: Diane B. Engel

Copyright © by Holt, Rinehart and Winston

All rights reserved. No part of this publication may be reproduced or transmitted in any form or by any means, electronic or mechanical, including photocopy, recording, or any information storage and retrieval system, without permission in writing from the publisher.

Teachers using HRW LIBRARY may photocopy blackline masters in complete pages in sufficient quantities for classroom use only and not for resale.

HRW is a registered trademark licensed to Holt, Rinehart and Winston.

Printed in the United States of America

ISBN 0-03-054052-6

3456 085 02 01

TABLE *of* CONTENTS

FOR THE TEACHER

Using This Study Guide 2

Tips for Classroom Management 3

Strategies for Inclusion 4

Assessment Options 5

About the Writer 6

About the Novel 7

Key Elements: Plot / Theme / Characters / Setting / Point of View / Foreshadowing 8–10

Resources Overview .... inside front cover	Answer Key 42–51

FOR THE STUDENT

Before You Read: Activities 11

Chapters 1–6: Making Meanings / Choices 12–13

Chapters 7–10: Making Meanings / Choices 14–15

Chapters 11–15: Making Meanings / Choices 16–17

Novel Projects: Cross-Curricular Connections / Multimedia and Internet Connections 18–19

Exploring the Connections: Making Meanings 20–22

    A Personal Note, by Paul Zindel 20

    Happy Birthday, by Toni Cade Bambara 20

    Abuela Invents the Zero, by Judith Ortiz Cofer 21

    Fifth Grade Autobiography, by Rita Dove 21

    Abuela, by Denise Alcalá 21

    Lineage, by Margaret Walker 21

    Niña, by Margarita Mondrus Engle 22

    My First Love, by Bill Cosby 22

Novel Notes: Issues 1–6 23–28

Reading Skills and Strategies Worksheets: Novel Organizer / Noting Settings /

    Responding to Quotations / Identifying Consequences 29–33

Literary Elements Worksheets: Point of View / Foreshadowing 34–35

Glossary 36

Vocabulary Worksheet 37

Test 38–41

Study Guide | **1**

Using This Study Guide

This Study Guide is intended to
- *help students become active and engaged readers*
- *deepen students' enjoyment and understanding of literature*
- *provide you with multiple options for guiding students through the novel and the Connections and for evaluating students' progress*

Most of the pages in this Study Guide are reproducible so that you can, if you choose, give students the opportunity to work independently.

Key Elements
- plot summary and analysis
- major themes
- character summaries
- notes on setting, point of view, and other literary elements

Making Meanings
- First Thoughts
- Shaping Interpretations
- Connecting with the Text
- Extending the Text
- Challenging the Text

A **Reading Check** focuses on review and comprehension.

The Worksheets
- **Reading Skills and Strategies Worksheets** focus on reading and critical-thinking strategies and skills.
- **Literary Elements Worksheets** guide students in considering and analyzing literary elements (discussed in **Key Elements**) important to understanding the novel.
- **Vocabulary Worksheets** provide practice with Vocabulary Words. Activities target synonyms, affixes, roots, context clues, and other vocabulary elements.

For the Teacher

About the Writer Biographical highlights supplement the author biography that appears in the HRW Library edition of this novel. Sidebars list works by and about the writer as resources for teaching and for students' research.

About the Novel A critical history summarizes responses to the novel, including excerpts from reviews. Sidebars suggest audiovisual and multimedia resources.

Key Elements Significant literary elements of the novel are introduced. These elements recur in the questions, activities, worksheets, and assessment tools.

For the Student: reproducible masters

Before You Read: Activities *(preparation for beginning the novel)* Motivating activities lead students to explore ideas and topics they will encounter in the novel.

Making Meanings *(for each section of the novel)* Questions move students from immediate personal response to high-level critical thinking.

Choices: Building Your Portfolio *(for each section of the novel)* The activities suggested here involve students in exploring different aspects of the novel on their own or collaboratively. The results may be included in a portfolio, developed further, or used as springboards for larger projects.

Novel Projects *(culminating activities)* Cross-Curricular, Multimedia, and Internet projects relate to the novel as a whole. Project ideas can be adapted for individual, pair, or group presentations.

Exploring the Connections *(a set of Making Meanings questions for each of the Connections readings)* Questions encourage students to relate the readings to the themes and topics of the novel.

Novel Notes *(multiple issues)* These one-page news sheets provide high-interest background information relating to historical, cultural, literary, and other elements of the novel. They are intended for distribution *after* students have begun the novel section the issue supplements.

Reading Skills and Strategies Worksheets *(one for each section of the novel, plus a Novel Organizer)*

Literary Elements Worksheets *(end of novel)*

Vocabulary Worksheets *(during or after reading)*

Glossary, with Vocabulary Words *(to use throughout the novel)* This list of words from the novel serves as a mini-dictionary that students may refer to as they read. **Highlighted Vocabulary Words** support vocabulary acquisition.

Test *(end of novel)* A mix of objective and short-answer questions covering the whole novel provides a traditional form of assessment. Essay questions consist of five optional writing prompts.

The Pigman

Tips for Classroom Management

Preparing Students for Reading
Set aside a time each week for talking about books. On the right are some ideas for introducing a novel and motivating students to pick it up and begin reading.

Reading and Responding
Book groups Although most students will read independently, discussions with classmates can enrich their reading enormously. This Study Guide suggests appropriate points to stop and talk about the story so far. At these stopping points, the **Making Meanings** questions can be used as discussion starters. Ask groups to keep a simple log of their discussions.

Full-class discussions Engage students by beginning the discussion with a question that encourages a personal response (see **First Thoughts** in **Making Meanings**). As students respond to the questions involving interpretation, invite them to support their inferences and conclusions with evidence from the text. Encourage a noncritical environment. Show your own enthusiasm for the novel—it's infectious!

Reader's logs Logs, journals, and notebooks offer an open and nonthreatening yet systematic mode for students to respond in writing to the novel. Making entries as they read can help students learn more about themselves as readers, monitor their own progress, and write more easily and fluently. Keeping logs can also enhance participation in small-group and class discussions of the novel. Consider dialogue journals in which two readers—a student and you, a classmate, or a family member—exchange thoughts about their reading. **Reader's Log** suggestions appear in each issue of **Novel Notes**.

Cooperative learning Small groups may meet both to discuss the novel and to plan and work on projects related to the novel (see ideas in **Choices** and in **Novel Projects**). Encourage full participation by making sure that each group member has a defined role and that the roles rotate so that the same student is not always the leader or the recorder, for example.

Projects While students' projects can extend into other content areas, they should always contribute to enriching and extending students' understanding of the novel itself. If students know when they begin the novel that presenting a project will be a part of their evaluation, they can begin early to brainstorm, discuss, and try out ideas. Project ideas can come from **Novel Notes**, from the **Choices** activities, from the **Novel Projects** ideas, and, of course, from the students themselves. Projects can be developed and presented by individuals, pairs, or groups.

Reflecting
When students finish the novel, they should not be left with a test as the culminating experience. Project presentations can be a kind of celebration, as can a concluding discussion. On the right are some ideas for a reflective discussion. They can be used in a whole-class environment, or small groups can choose certain questions to answer and share their conclusions (or their disagreements) with the class.

Ideas for Introducing the Novel
- Give a brief book talk to arouse students' curiosity and interest (see **About the Novel** for ideas).
- Play or show a segment of an audio, film, or video version of the book or an interview with the writer.
- Present high-interest biographical information about the writer (see **About the Writer** in this Study Guide and the biographical sketch at the end of the HRW Library edition of this novel).
- Read aloud a passage from the novel that arouses your own interest, and elicit predictions, inferences, and speculations from students.
- Lead a focused class discussion or suggest activities that (1) draw on students' prior knowledge or (2) lead them to generate their own ideas about a significant topic or theme they will encounter in the novel (see **Before You Read).**

Reader's Log Starters
- When I began reading this book, I thought…
- My favorite part, so far, is…
- I predict that…
- I like the way the writer…
- I'd like to ask the writer…
- If I had written this book, I would have…
- This [character, incident, idea] reminds me of…
- This book made me think about…
- This book made me realize…

Questions for Reflection
- What was your favorite part of the book (and why)?
- If you could be one of the characters, who would it be (and why)?
- Would you or wouldn't you recommend this book to a friend (and why)?
- What is the most important thing about this book?
- Would you change the ending? If not, what makes it work? If yes, what changes would you make?
- If you could have a conversation with the writer, what would you say or ask?

Strategies for Inclusion

Each set of activities has been developed to meet special student interests, abilities, and learning styles. Because the questions and activities in this Study Guide are directed to the students, there are no labels to indicate the types of learners they target. However, in each Before You Read, Choices, *and* Novel Projects *page, you will find activities to meet the needs of*

- *less proficient readers*
- *students acquiring English*
- *advanced students*

The activities and projects have been prepared to accommodate these different learning styles:

- *auditory/musical*
- *interpersonal*
- *intrapersonal*
- *kinesthetic*
- *logical/mathematical*
- *verbal/linguistic*
- *visual/spatial*

Using the Study Guide Questions and Activities

Encourage students to adapt the suggestions given in the Study Guide to fit their own learning styles and interests. It is important to remember that students are full of surprises, and a question or activity that is challenging to an advanced student can also be handled successfully by students who are less proficient readers. The high interest level, flexibility, and variety of these questions and activities make them appropriate for a range of students.

Students should be encouraged to vary the types of activities they choose so that the same student is not regularly selecting writing or researching activities over those involving speaking, art, and performing, and vice versa. Individual and group work should also alternate, so that students have the opportunity to work on their own and as part of collaborative learning groups.

Working in Pairs and Groups

When students with varying abilities, cultural backgrounds, and learning styles work together, they can arrive at a deeper understanding of both the novel and one another.

Reading pairs can stop and check each other's responses to the novel at frequent intervals.

Students from different cultural groups can interview one another about how certain situations, character interactions, character motivations, and so on would be viewed in their home cultures.

Visualizing and Performing

Students who have difficulty with writing or with presenting their ideas orally can demonstrate their understanding of the novel in a variety of ways:

- making cluster diagrams or sketching their ideas
- creating tableaux showing where characters are in relation to one another during a scene, their poses or stances, and their facial expressions
- creating thought balloons with drawings or phrases that show what a character is thinking at a given moment
- drawing their own thoughts in thought balloons above a sketched self-portrait
- listing or drawing images that come to mind as they read or hear a certain section or passage of the novel
- making a comic-book version of the novel (with or without words)
- coming to class as a character in the novel

Assessment Options

Perhaps the most important goal of assessment is to inform instruction. As you monitor the degree to which your students understand and engage with the novel, you will naturally modify your instructional plan. The frequency and balance of class and small-group discussion, the time allowed for activities, and the extent to which direct teaching of reading skills and strategies, literary elements, or vocabulary is appropriate can all be planned on the basis of your ongoing assessment of your students' needs.

Several forms of assessment are particularly appropriate for work with the novel:

Observing and note taking Anecdotal records that reflect both the degree and the quality of students' participation in class and small-group discussions and activities will help you target areas in which coaching or intervention is appropriate. Because communication skills are such an integral part of working with the novel in a classroom setting, it is appropriate to evaluate the process of making meaning in this social context.

Involving yourself with dialogue journals and letters You may want to exchange notes with students instead of, or in addition to, encouraging them to keep reader's logs. A powerful advantage of this strategy is that at the same time you have the opportunity to evaluate students' responses, you can make a significant difference in the quality of the response. When students are aware that their comments are valued (and addressed to a real audience, an audience that writes back), they often wake up to the significance of what they are reading and begin to make stronger connections between the text and their own lives.

Agreeing on criteria for evaluation If evaluation is to be fair, it must be predictable. As students propose and plan an activity or project, collaborate with them to set up the criteria by which their work will be evaluated, and be consistent in applying only those criteria.

Encouraging self-evaluation and goal setting When students are partners with you in creating criteria for evaluation, they can apply those criteria to their own work. You might ask them to rate themselves on a simple scale of 1, 2, or 3 for each of the criteria and to arrive at an overall score. Students can then set goals based on self-evaluation.

Peer evaluation Students can participate in evaluating one another's demonstrations and presentations, basing their evaluations upon a previously established set of standards. Modeling a peer-evaluation session will help students learn this method, and a chart or checklist can guide peer discussion. Encourage students to be objective, sensitive, courteous, and constructive in their comments.

Keeping portfolios If you are in an environment where portfolios contain only carefully chosen samples of students' writing, you may want to introduce a second, "working," portfolio and negotiate grades with students after examining all or selected items from these portfolios.

Opportunities for Assessment

The suggestions in this Study Guide provide multiple opportunities for assessment across a range of skills:

- demonstrating reading comprehension
- keeping reader's logs
- listening and speaking
- working in groups—both discussion and activity-oriented
- planning, developing, and presenting a final project
- acquiring vocabulary
- taking tests

Questions for Self-evaluation and Goal Setting

- What are the three most important things I learned in my work with this novel?
- How will I follow up with these so that I remember them?
- What was the most difficult part of working with this novel?
- How did I deal with the difficulty, and what would I do differently?
- What two goals will I work toward in my [reading/writing/group work, etc.]?
- What steps will I take to achieve those goals?

Items for a "Working" Portfolio

- reading records
- drafts of written work and project plans
- audio- and videotapes of presentations
- notes on discussions
- reminders of cooperative projects, such as planning and discussion notes
- artwork
- objects and mementos connected with themes and topics in the novel
- other evidence of engagement with the book

*For help with establishing and maintaining portfolio assessment, examine the **Portfolio Management System** in **Elements of Literature**.*

About the Writer — Paul Zindel

More on Zindel

"Paul Zindel." **Bantam Doubleday Dell Books for Young Readers Teacher's Resource Center/authors + illustrators index.** Available online at http://www.bdd.com/teachers/zind.html with a link to a RealAudio message from the author.

"Zindel, Paul." **Something About the Author,** Volume 58, pp. 198–209. Detroit: Gale Research, 1990. Detailed overview of Zindel's writings.

Zindel, Paul. "Journey to Meet the Pigman." **The ALAN Review,** Volume 22, No. 1 (Fall 1994). Available online at http://scholar.lib.vt.edu/ejournals/ALAN/fall94/Zindel.html. Zindel describes the life experiences behind *The Pigman.*

For an expanded autobiographical account, see **The Pigman & Me** (New York: HarperCollins, 1992).

Also by Zindel

The Amazing and Death-Defying Diary of Eugene Dingman. New York: Harper & Row, 1987. Through a series of diary entries, this narrative describes a teenager's search for a father figure.

A Begonia for Miss Applebaum. New York: Harper & Row, 1989. Teenagers Henry and Zelda become companions of their favorite teacher as she faces a terminal illness.

Loch: A Novel. New York: HarperCollins, 1994. Loch Perkins and his sister Zaidee accompany their father on an expedition to prove that a mythical monster actually exists.

The Pigman's Legacy. New York: Harper & Row, 1980. In this sequel to *The Pigman,* John and Lorraine find adventure and a chance to make up for past mistakes when they discover a stranger hiding in Mr. Pignati's house.

A biography of Paul Zindel appears in The Pigman, HRW *Library edition. You may wish to share this additional biographical information with your students.*

Although Paul Zindel grew up in a home without books, his active imagination and need to express himself led him to write his first play while still a teenager (after a brief, frustrating attempt at acting in school plays). His efforts won him a prize in a playwriting contest sponsored by the American Cancer Society. He continued writing plays during the ten years he taught at Tottenville High School on Staten Island. The best-known of these—*The Effect of Gamma Rays on Man-in-the-Moon Marigolds*—opened to critical acclaim at Houston's Alley Theater in 1964, halfway through his teaching career.

For both his plays and novels, Zindel's teaching experiences have served as a springboard for many characters, plots, and themes. His mother served as the inspiration for both Beatrice in *The Effect of Gamma Rays on Man-in-the-Moon Marigolds* and Lorraine's mother, Mrs. Jensen, in *The Pigman.* He confirms the autobiographical nature of his work by noting that whenever he is in the audience of a production of *The Effect of Gamma Rays on Man-in-the-Moon Marigolds,* he laughs and cries louder than anyone else.

Zindel's works, among the earliest books of young adult fiction, filled a void. The author says that when he began reading books written for teenagers, he saw little in them that reflected the interests or lives of real teenagers. He writes primarily for teenagers who do not enjoy reading; in his teaching experience he saw that these were the students who had difficulty in school and who missed out on a broad range of ideas.

Although Zindel has been criticized for focusing his young adult novels on desperate teenagers and the often antagonistic adults in their lives, he stands by his work. Since many young people feel the need to rebel in order to find their identity, putting themselves in the shoes of Zindel's teenaged characters gives them something to rebel against. Depicting adults in an unflattering light also helps Zindel show his readers that he is on their side in the struggle toward adulthood.

About the Novel

The Pigman

Encouraged by a suggestion from editor Charlotte Zolotow, Paul Zindel used fiction to explore what he considers the difficult, often painful journey that most humans experience between the ages of twelve and nineteen. The first product of these explorations was this award-winning novel.

CRITICAL COMMENT

> *The Pigman,* like its successors, has caused controversy, especially among critics. A book review by Diane Farrell in *The Horn Book* stated, "Few books that have been written for young people are as cruelly truthful about the human condition." Lavinia Russ described *The Pigman* as "astonishingly good." In *The New York Times,* however, Josh Greenfeld wrote: "How do you reach the young, the teen-agers? In books, as in life, I do not know. But neither, I think, does Mr. Zindel. For I do know that fiction must offer truth in the guise of illusion, not illusion instead of the truth."

The Pigman should pose no problems for students reading at or above grade level. The book does, however, contain scenes of mild violence, disruptive classroom behavior, teenage smoking and drinking, and ruminations about death. The only adult in the novel who provides a positive role model is the Pigman. (The narrators generally are quite biased against adults—something you may wish to discuss with students.) The book is best suited to emotionally mature students who can place adult themes in perspective. Despite the gritty subject matter (or perhaps because of it), the novel remains one of the first and most popular in the genre of young adult literature ever written.

Awards and Honors

ALA Best Young Adult Book

The Horn Book Honor Book

Child Study Association of America Children's Book of the Year

For Viewing

The Pigman. Miller-Brody/Random House, 1978. Filmstrip with cassette, with screenplay written by Paul Zindel.

For Listening

The Pigman & Me. Recorded Books, 1994. A three-cassette memoir of Zindel and the "real" Pigman.

Key Elements — *The Pigman*

Plot

Chapters 1–6 The troublemaking John and the unattractive Lorraine make prank phone calls with their friends. The response from Mr. Angelo Pignati ("the Pigman") leads John and Lorraine to his door under the pretense of being charity workers. Mr. Pignati, who explains that his wife is in California, teaches the teenagers a memory trick and shows them his collection of pig figurines. Over Lorraine's objections, John uses Mr. Pignati's "charity donation" to buy beer and cigarettes. Later, Lorraine endures her mother's questions and complaints. The next day, John and Lorraine skip school to meet Bobo the baboon, the Pigman's favorite animal at the zoo.

Chapters 7–10 John thinks about life's meaning at a cemetery, then goes home to a depressing Conlan family dinner. The teenagers continue to visit Mr. Pignati at his house, where John discovers the bill for Mrs. Pignati's funeral. Mr. Pignati leads the teens through Beekman's Department Store and buys them gifts. When Norton threatens to rob the Pigman's house, John knows that he will kill Norton if he hurts Pignati. Lorraine describes a typical conversation with her distrustful mother. One night, John and Lorraine admit to the Pigman that they are not charity workers. In turn, Mr. Pignati confesses that his wife has died. They all let off steam by skating through the house—until the Pigman collapses from a heart attack.

Chapters 11–15 At the hospital, Mr. Pignati asks Lorraine and John (who pose as his children) to take care of Bobo; he also gives them the keys to his house. The couple share a romantic dinner at his house dressed in clothes they find there. As time goes on, though, they find themselves quarreling. Lorraine has a nightmare about the "pig room" that she feels is an omen of death. John throws a party, and some of the Pigman's most cherished possessions, including his pigs, are ruined. Mr. Pignati returns home while the party is in progress. John and Lorraine are escorted home by the police. To make up for their awful behavior, the teenagers propose a group visit to see Bobo. At the zoo, they find out Bobo has died, and Mr. Pignati drops dead of a heart attack. John and Lorraine leave the zoo saddened but with a new sense of responsibility.

Plot Elements Lorraine and John's conflicts with parents and authority figures drive them toward their friendship with the Pigman. The novel's climax, when Mr. Pignati returns from the hospital to find that

Key Elements (continued)

The Pigman

John and Lorraine have betrayed his trust, is sandwiched between two smaller climaxes in which Mr. Pignati suffers heart attacks. In the novel's denouement, Lorraine and John struggle with their role in the Pigman's death and the impact he has had on their lives.

Theme

Students will see the following **themes,** or main ideas, developed in detail in *The Pigman*.

The Power of Love In Angelo Pignati, Paul Zindel has created a character whose loving personality exerts a powerful positive influence on the somewhat wayward John and Lorraine. Through their experience with the Pigman, the teenagers discover love for each other as well as for this unusual, lonely man.

Self-Discovery Lorraine and John want to break free but fear the future because their parents present negative models of adulthood. The Pigman, though, presents a more positive way of looking at maturity and freedom, and his example helps John and Lorraine learn the importance of responsibility for people they care about.

Among Generations The author realistically portrays teenagers who feel trapped and isolated. Lorraine and John learn through their relationship with the Pigman, though, that an enjoyable life doesn't end with adulthood. In turn, the Pigman regains a feeling of happiness and belonging through the teenagers' energy and sense of adventure.

Characters

Students will meet the following major **characters** in *The Pigman*.

John Conlan is one of the narrators of the novel. He is a handsome, imaginative high school student with a rebellious streak. He dreams of becoming an actor.

Lorraine Jensen, the novel's other narrator, is John's best friend. Highly verbal, sensitive, and earnest, she wants to be a writer.

The Pigman, Angelo Pignati, is a retired electrician whom John describes as being in his late fifties. His nickname comes from the pig figurines that he and his wife collected. A lonely widower, he befriends Lorraine and John.

Dennis Kobin and **Norton Kelly** are troublemakers from John and Lorraine's school.

Make a Connection

Discuss the attitudes that teenagers have toward adults, especially senior citizens. What do teenagers expect of older people they meet, for example? What activities might they both enjoy? How might they benefit from each others' company? Invite students to see how their answers are reflected in the **themes** of *The Pigman*.

Connecting with Elements of Literature

You can use *The Pigman* to extend students' examination of the themes and topics presented in *Elements of Literature*.

- *Introductory Course:* "Unforgettable Personalities," Collection Two
- *First Course:* "Do the Right Thing," Collection Three
- *Second Course:* "From Generation to Generation," Collection Two

Key Elements (continued)   *The Pigman*

Make a Connection

Have students describe an urban zoo setting. What kinds of sights, sounds, and smells might they find in such a setting? What emotions or ideas arise when students consider this setting? What events do they predict might happen in this setting?

Make a Connection

Ask for two volunteers to take turns telling about how your class began today (without hearing each other's version of events). Have the class discuss how the stories were similar or different in terms of tone, interpretation, and details. Ask students how they think a story might change when the narrator changes.

*A **Literary Elements Worksheet** that focuses on point of view appears on page 34 of this Study Guide.*

Make a Connection

Ask students to identify examples of **foreshadowing** in other books or films with which they are familiar. Encourage students to read *The Pigman* actively, taking notes about details and events that they think may be clues foretelling what will happen later. Have them make predictions about later events in their notes, then confirm or adjust their predictions as they continue reading.

*A **Literary Elements Worksheet** that focuses on foreshadowing appears on page 35 of this Study Guide.*

Bore and **the Old Lady** are John's nicknames for his parents. Although they respect their son's imagination, they don't know how to cope with him.

Mrs. Jensen, a private nurse, is Lorraine's mother. (She and Mr. Jensen separated, and Mr. Jensen died, before the story begins.) She is unhappy most of the time and often acts selfishly.

Setting

The events of *The Pigman* take place on Staten Island, an island in New York Bay. Although Staten Island is part of New York City, it more closely resembles a suburb or small town because of its relative isolation. The time of this story is the late 1960s.

Point of View

Because Lorraine and John take turns telling the story of their relationship with the Pigman, the story is told from an alternating **first-person point of view.** When readers come across the personal pronoun *I*, they should be aware that the thoughts, feelings, and knowledge of the character who is narrating are being expressed.

Foreshadowing

Foreshadowing is the use of hints or clues to suggest events that will occur later in a **plot**. Details that relate to foreshadowing can help build **suspense** or anxiety in a reader and can influence the **atmosphere** or **mood** of the story.

From the beginning chapters of *The Pigman,* Lorraine talks about omens—occurrences that seem to foretell a future event. For example, Lorraine interprets her nightmare about the "pig room" as an omen of death, foreshadowing the death of Mr. Pignati. At every turn of the page, the reader expects the awful "something" that the earlier conversation foreshadowed—and, eventually, it happens.

Before You Read

The Pigman

Activities

BUILDING ON PRIOR KNOWLEDGE

My Generation

The Pigman takes place in the late sixties. What do you know about that time? With some classmates, make a comparison-and-contrast chart about details of contemporary life then and now. You might want to give examples such as political figures, news stories, tastes in music, clothing styles, movies, and television programs. (To gather details, check an encyclopedia or history book, or interview adults you know who remember that time well.) Post your charts around the classroom and refer to them as you read.

SOLVING PROBLEMS

Pressure Plan

Like the characters in *The Pigman*, teenagers often face situations that involve peer pressure. With your classmates, brainstorm for a list of ways in which teens can deal with peer-pressure situations. Add as many ideas as you can to the following list:

- Ask questions to make sure that you understand the situation.
- Communicate your feelings without criticizing the other person.
- Ask your peers for advice.
- If you cannot agree, walk away instead of fighting.

As you read Paul Zindel's novel, decide which of the ideas the characters use—or need to use.

MAKING A PERSONAL CONNECTION

What's in a Nickname?

Flash, Hollywood, Stretch—what do these terms have in common? They are all nicknames. Several characters in *The Pigman* have nicknames. With a partner or small group, talk about nicknames. How are they chosen? What does a nickname say about the person who has that nickname—and about the person who gave it to him or her? Review your answers as you get to know the people in *The Pigman*.

MAKING PREDICTIONS

Oath My Goodness!

Just before *The Pigman* begins, there is "The Oath," signed by the novel's two narrators. Read it and discuss these questions with a partner:

- What facts do you learn about John and Lorraine from these few sentences?
- Why do you think they call their story "this memorial epic"?
- Why do you think they feel they have to take an oath before telling their story?

Use this activity to make some predictions about the novel and then see if they come true.

Novel Notes

Use **Novel Notes, Issue 1**

- to find out more about some of the topics and themes in *The Pigman*
- to get ideas for writing activities and other projects that will take you deeper into the book

Chapters 1–6

The Pigman

Making Meanings

First Thoughts

1. Would you want Lorraine or John as a friend? Why or why not?

Shaping Interpretations

2. John Conlan is the **narrator** of Chapters 1, 3, and 5. Lorraine Jensen narrates Chapters 2, 4, and 6. Contrast the ways in which they tell their shared story. (For example, how does their **tone,** or attitude toward their subject, differ?)

> **READING CHECK**
>
> These first chapters introduce several **characters** and their nicknames. Identify the character to which each name relates. Then, explain the reason for each nickname.
>
> **a.** the Bathroom Bomber
> **b.** the Cricket
> **c.** the Marshmallow Kid
> **d.** the Bore
> **e.** the Pigman

3. Why do you think John pulls pranks on strangers, friends, and even his own family?

4. When they contact Mr. Pignati, Lorraine calls herself "Miss Truman" and John calls himself "Mr. Wandermeyer." Why might these names be **ironic**—that is, having a meaning that Lorraine and John do not realize?

5. In your opinion, why does Mr. Pignati treat John and Lorraine generously?

6. How do you think John, Lorraine, and Mr. Pignati feel when they all begin to howl like monkeys? Why might this **scene** be important to the story?

Connecting with the Text

7. Suppose that you could step into the story at this point and ask any of the characters a question. To whom would you speak? What would you ask?

Extending the Text

8. Almost everyone you meet in these first chapters acts dishonestly. Why do you think people sometimes lie, not only in the novel, but also in real life? Explain.

Challenging the Text

9. Even before you meet Mr. Pignati, you find out that he will die before the story is over. In your opinion, should the writer have given that information away so early? Why or why not?

Chapters 1–6 *(continued)*

The Pigman

Choices: Building Your Portfolio

COOPERATIVE LEARNING

Getting Along

Both Lorraine and John have trouble getting along with people. Review Chapters 1–6 with a few classmates. Look for examples of missed communication and misunderstanding between these two **characters** and the people around them. As you find examples, discuss what each character could do to make things better. For example, was there a better way for John to respond to his father's anger? What should Lorraine have done when her mother wanted her to skip school to clean house? Have a recorder write down your group's suggestions and then share them with the class.

ART

Let Me Illustrate . . .

Create a comic strip of an important or interesting **scene** in this section of the novel. Your comic strip should have at least four frames and include **dialogue**. Feel free to use captions to explain any action in your scene that might be difficult to depict. Then, share your comic strip with the class by explaining it aloud or hanging it on a bulletin board.

BRAIN POWER

Thanks for the Memory

Try out the method Mr. Pignati uses to memorize ten objects in Chapter 5. (You might even want to use it to remember important items in *The Pigman*.) Have a classmate or two name ten items and test your memory with this visual technique. Then, turn the tables and test them on a list of ten items.

CREATIVE WRITING

Dear Diary, . . .

This novel shows us what John and Lorraine are thinking, but what about Mr. Pignati? Step into his shoes for a moment and write two diary entries. In character, share your thoughts about (1) meeting the two young "charity workers," and (2) the visit to the zoo with them. Decide how much you think the Pigman understands about his young friends. Have him share the feelings behind his smile and twinkling eyes. How does this activity help you understand the novel's characters?

Consider This . . .

His own life is so boring when measured against his daydreams that he can't stand it, so he makes up things to pretend it's exciting.

Lorraine makes this comment about John. In your opinion, is she right about John's life being boring? about the reasons that he "makes up things"?

Writing Follow-up: Problem-Solving

Explain two pieces of advice you might give John to help him enjoy life more. How would following your advice benefit John?

Novel Notes

Use **Novel Notes, Issue 2**

- to find out more about some of the topics and themes in Chapters 1–6
- to get ideas for writing activities and other projects related to *The Pigman*

Chapters 7–10

The Pigman

Making Meanings

First Thoughts

1. Respond to Chapters 7–10 by completing these sentences.
   - The part that made me happiest was . . .
   - The part that made me saddest was . . .
   - The part that surprised me most was . . .

> **READING CHECK**
>
> Chapters 7 and 9 are narrated by John; Chapters 8 and 10 are narrated by Lorraine. Working with a partner, choose one of the **narrators** and summarize the events from the narrator's chapters in this section of the novel.

Shaping Interpretations

2. Think about John's dinner with his parents. How does that **scene** affect the way you think about the Conlans? Explain.

3. One of the **themes** of this novel is "The Power of Love." How do you see that theme at work in the life of Mr. Pignati?

4. The **atmosphere** or **mood** of a story is the "feeling" it expresses. In Chapter 10, the atmosphere or mood at Mr. Pignati's home changes dramatically—and more than once. Describe those changes.

5. In a story, **dynamic characters** change because of their experiences. At this point, how do you know that John is a dynamic character?

Connecting with the Text

6. Mr. Pignati has a real taste for the unusual. Does he remind you of anyone you know or have read about? Explain.

Extending the Text

7. Lorraine says, "I've always wondered about those cases where a man and wife die within a short time of each other." Why do you think this sometimes happens?

Challenging the Text

8. The novel contains some "real-life" writings such as a bill, an advice column, and a psychological game. Do these things get in the way of your reading, or do they help? How do they affect your understanding of the story?

Chapters 7–10 (continued)

The Pigman

Choices: Building Your Portfolio

COOPERATIVE LEARNING

Rite of Passage
From Chapters 7–10, choose a short passage that you found memorable. In a group, take turns reading aloud your passages and giving your reactions to the passages that you hear. For example, which were the most surprising or upsetting? Which expressed a thought in a unique or interesting way? If any group members have chosen the same passage, see if you can figure out why.

COMPARISON

Just Like Me?
How well do you know yourself? One way to find out is to compare yourself to the **characters** you meet in a book. On a sheet of paper, make two columns. In the left-hand column, list ways in which you think you are similar to John or Lorraine (or even Mr. Pignati) in your thoughts, speech, and behavior. In the right-hand column, list ways in which you are different.

DRAMA

Afternoon at the Improv
Work with some classmates to improvise a key **scene** from Chapters 7–10 (for example, John's dinner with his parents or the scene in the sports department of Beekman's). You will need to be familiar enough with the scene to act it out in character, but you do not need to memorize dialogue from the book. Your words, movements, facial expressions, and gestures should make clear what your **character** is thinking during the scene and reveal his or her personality. If possible, videotape the scene.

CREATIVE WRITING

Conlan Conversation
Do you think that John's parents are really as unlikable as Lorraine and John make them appear? With a partner, write a **dialogue** between John's parents, Mr. and Mrs. Conlan. Have it take place after dinner and after John has left the house. In their conversation, have them share their hopes and concerns about John. If you wish, act out the dialogue for the class and ask for comments. How does the dialogue support or contradict John and Lorraine's opinions of this couple?

Consider This . . .
"Look at me, world! Look at my life and energy and how glad I am to be alive!"

Lorraine imagines that this is how John feels as he roller-skates through Beekman's. What makes John glad to be alive? What makes him feel a lack of energy or excitement in life?

Writing Follow-up: Reflecting

What makes you glad to be alive? When the world looks at you, how does it see your life and energy?

Novel Notes

Use **Novel Notes, Issue 3**

- to find out more about some of the topics and themes in Chapters 7–10
- to get ideas for writing activities and other projects related to *The Pigman*

Study Guide | **15**

Chapters 11–15

The Pigman

Making Meanings

First Thoughts
1. Describe your feelings about the ending of *The Pigman*.

Shaping Interpretations
2. Why do you think John and Lorraine quarrel after their kiss?

3. In your opinion, how does the party at the Pigman's house change the direction of this story?

4. When Lorraine and John call Mr. Pignati, he does not answer their questions quickly. What **internal conflict**—what clash of thoughts and feelings—might make him hesitate?

5. Why do you think Bobo's death hits Mr. Pignati so hard? What do you think the baboon **symbolized,** or represented, to him?

6. What are two lessons you think Lorraine and John learn when Mr. Pignati dies?

Connecting with the Text
7. Suppose you had been at the party. Could you have said or done anything to keep things from getting out of hand?

Extending the Text
8. How do you think people from different generations—like John and Lorraine and Mr. Pignati—can learn to understand and appreciate one another better?

Challenging the Text
9. Did Mr. Pignati have to die in order for Lorraine and John to learn the lessons they did? Explain your answer.

> **READING CHECK**
>
> Retell this last part of the novel as a "story round." With a group of classmates, take turns telling major details and events from Chapters 11–15. If you wish, you might also mention details and events from earlier chapters that are related to what takes place in this section.

Chapters 11–15 *(continued)*

The Pigman

Choices: Building Your Portfolio

COOPERATIVE LEARNING

A *Pigman* Quiz

Form a group to discuss one of the three sections of *The Pigman*. In your group, write five questions for your section about **characters**, **plot** details, **themes** of the novel, its **setting**, and so on. Write each question and its answer on an index card—five cards in all. With your teacher's help, gather the cards and organize the class into two teams. The teacher or a student moderator can read each question aloud and keep score.

SENSORY DESCRIPTION

Live It Up!

John and Lorraine's party turns out very badly. The **scene** itself, however, is very vivid. How does Zindel make the party come alive for you? Make a word web for each of the five senses: taste, hearing, touch, smell, and sight. List words and phrases from that scene that appeal to each of these senses.

SPEAKING AND LISTENING

Judging Mrs. Jensen

We learn more about Lorraine's mother in Chapters 12 and 14. The picture that we get of her is a harsh one, but we also discover some reasons for her behavior. With a partner or a few classmates, discuss these questions:

- Why has Mrs. Jensen become such a sad, selfish, suspicious person?
- Does she have any good qualities at all?
- Could a person like her change?
- How should Lorraine deal with her?

CREATIVE WRITING

"Goodbye, Mr. Pignati"

A eulogy is a speech in honor of someone who has died. Write a eulogy for Angelo Pignati. Tell about his life, but focus on his personality and the influence he had on other people. Include details from the novel and, if you wish, write it as if you were Lorraine or John. For an extra challenge, try to match the style of the novel and have both characters say something about their friend.

Consider This . . .

Our life would be what we made of it—nothing more, nothing less.

These are John's words at the end of the novel. Do you agree? Why or why not?

Writing Follow-up: Cause and Effect

As a result of their relationship with Mr. Pignati, John and Lorraine have learned to take responsibility for their actions. What effects do you think this change will have on their relationships with others and on the rest of their lives?

Novel Notes

Use **Novel Notes, Issue 4**

- to find out more about some of the topics and themes in Chapters 11–15
- to get ideas for writing activities and other projects related to *The Pigman*

Study Guide

Novel Projects

The Pigman

Cross-Curricular Connections

ART

Art and Soul

Illustrate one or more scenes from *The Pigman* in the medium of your choice. Whether you decide to draw, paint, sculpt, or create some other kind of artwork, try to capture the "soul"—the important ideas and feelings—in the part of the novel that you are illustrating. You might explain your artistic choices in a presentation or get together with some classmates and create a "*Pigman* Art Gallery" of your finished pieces.

SOCIAL STUDIES

About Ageism

At first, Lorraine and John see Mr. Pignati as just a "nice old man." Before long, though, they find that he is much more than that. To put it another way, they start to put aside their *ageism*—their prejudiced ideas about older people. How do people reveal ageism in everyday life? First, consider how ageism affects you; for example, notice how people act toward you and other people your age. How is this different from the way you see parents, teachers, or other adults treated? Then, consider the attitudes you and other young people have about the elderly. How do you think these attitudes might affect older people? Make a chart comparing stereotypes about young and old people based on your own ideas and interviews with a variety of other people.

HEALTH

The Heart of the Matter

Mr. Pignati seems to be recovering from his heart attack. Within a few days, however, he has dropped dead from a second attack. How could that have happened? How could he have developed heart trouble in the first place? Interview a health-care professional, or search on the Internet or in the library for information on the causes of heart disease. Find out how people "at risk" can lessen the chance of a heart attack. Prepare and present an oral report identifying three things people can do to reduce their risks of heart attacks.

SCIENCE

Shrinking Heads

In Chapter 5, John accuses Lorraine, "You think you're the perfect headshrinker with all those psychology books you read. . . ." The word *psychology* means "the science of human behavior and the mind." What, though, does a psychologist—a "headshrinker"—do? Do some research to find the answer to that question. You might also want to find out how a person trains to become a psychologist and what the difference is between psychology and psychiatry. As you share your findings in an oral or written report, offer your opinion on this question: How might Lorraine's interest in psychology help her as a writer?

Novel Projects (continued)

The Pigman

Multimedia and Internet Connections

NOTE: Check with your teacher about school policies on accessing Internet sites. If a Web site named here is not available, use key words to locate a similar site.

SCRIPT WRITING: TELEVISION

The Pigman on the Air

With four or five classmates, plan an adaptation of *The Pigman* as a televised play. Think about your options; for example, will you film on location in Staten Island or use a set? Also think about how you might show the characters' thoughts—in the cases of John and Lorraine, a very important element in the novel. Will you have them speak their minds, will you use a narrator, or will you let viewers infer the thoughts from the characters' actions? Outline a script or create a storyboard for part of the novel. After you present your ideas to the class, have the class as a whole discuss the differences between your televised play and the novel.

SOUNDTRACK: MUSIC

A Sound Idea

If *The Pigman* were a film, what would its soundtrack be like? Remember: Lorraine and John are teenagers in the late sixties, and Angelo Pignati has an Italian heritage. What kinds of music would reflect those details? Choose two or three pieces of music that could be part of a soundtrack for the film. You might use popular songs, classical music, or folk music. Try your best to include at least one piece for John and Lorraine and one piece for Mr. Pignati. As you share the music with the class, explain how you think it represents various characters, various events in the plot, or various themes of the novel.

LETTER WRITING: INTERNET

Pigman Pen Pals

Do you have a pen pal? Here is a Web site that can match you up with one:

Pen Pal Planet
http://www.epix.net/~ppplanet/page12.html

Browsing might lead you to other sites like these.

Once you find a pen pal, write him or her a letter. Write about yourself, your school, and the book that you have just read—*The Pigman*. Ask your pen pal about his or her school and the books that he or she has been reading. When you get an answer, write back. Who knows—Paul Zindel's book may help you find a lifelong friend!

SHOPPING: INTERNET

Gourmets in Cyberspace

Mr. Pignati loves to shop in the gourmet food section of Beekman's Department Store. Today, though, he might enjoy shopping for gourmet foods electronically. See what delicacies you can find online. Browse, using a keyword such as *gourmet,* and visit some of the Web sites that interest you. Make a list of foods that the Pigman might buy and share with his young friends. How much would he spend if he bought everything on your list?

For an extra challenge, do some browsing to find some places on the Internet where you could view and purchase pig figurines. (They're out there!)

Study Guide | **19**

Exploring the Connections

Making Meanings

A Personal Note

Novel Notes
See **Issue 5**

1. What are your impressions of Paul Zindel? Is he what you expected? Explain.

2. What does Zindel mean when he compares an "honest" novel to a dream?

3. Review what Zindel says about the **characters** who are parents in *The Pigman*. How do his comments affect the way you think about those characters?

4. If you wanted to be a professional writer, what advice do you think Zindel would give you?

5. What are some of the ideas that you would include in a letter to Paul Zindel about *The Pigman*?

> **READING CHECK**
>
> Name a real-life memory that Paul Zindel relates to each of the following **characters** in *The Pigman*.
>
> a. John
> b. Lorraine
> c. Lorraine's mother
> d. Norton
> e. the Pigman

Happy Birthday

Novel Notes
See **Issue 5**

1. How do your thoughts about Ollie change as you read "Happy Birthday"?

2. How is the **title** of this story **ironic**—that is, meaning something other than you would expect?

3. What is the **point of view** of this story? How would the story be different if Ollie were the **narrator?**

4. In what ways is "Happy Birthday" like *The Pigman*?

5. Why do you think birthday celebrations are very important to some people and unimportant to others?

> **READING CHECK**
>
> a. Where and when is "Happy Birthday" set?
> b. Who is Ollie Larkins, and what problem does she face?

20 | *The Pigman*

Exploring the Connections (continued)

Making Meanings

Abuela Invents the Zero

Novel Notes See **Issue 6**

1. With whose feelings do you sympathize more—Connie's or Abuela's? Why?

2. What words or phrases would you use to describe the **character** of Connie? of Abuela?

3. "Among Generations" is an important **theme** in *The Pigman*. What connection do you see between that theme and the **title** of this story?

4. Which of the **narrators** in *The Pigman* sounds more like Connie—Lorraine or John? Explain.

5. The story ends as Connie thinks about what has happened. Are you disappointed that the story doesn't go on to show her doing anything about her feelings? Why or why not?

> **READING CHECK**
>
> a. Why has Abuela come from the Island (Puerto Rico) for a visit?
>
> b. Why is Connie embarrassed to take her to church?
>
> c. Why is Abuela upset with Connie after church?

Fifth Grade Autobiography / Abuela / Lineage

Novel Notes See **Issue 6**

1. Which of these poems do you like best? Why?

2. What qualities do the grandparents in these poems have, according to the **speakers**?

3. How do the poems differ in **tone** or attitude?

4. Which of these poems reminds you most of your grandparents or another older adult you know? Explain.

5. Think about *The Pigman*. In general, do these poems remind you more of John or of Lorraine? Why?

> **READING CHECK**
>
> For each of these three poems, write one sentence that you think expresses the **main idea** of that poem. Exchange your sentences with a partner and compare.

Study Guide | **21**

Exploring the Connections (continued)

Making Meanings

Niña

Novel Notes
See **Issue 6**

1. How do you feel about Niña when this story ends? How do you feel about the narrator?

2. In your opinion, why does the narrator disobey her mother's instructions? What might she hope to gain by disobeying?

3. Compare the narrator's attitude toward Niña with Lorraine and John's attitude toward the Pigman.

4. What **moral,** or lesson about life, do "Niña" and *The Pigman* seem to share?

5. Imagine that you are a Cuban cousin of the narrator, about the same age as she is. What would you think of this American cousin from Los Angeles? Why?

READING CHECK

a. What three instructions do the girls receive? Which ones does the **narrator** disobey?

b. What is wrong with Niña? What happens to her?

My First Love

Novel Notes
See **Issue 5**

1. Did you think that this true story was funny? Why or why not?

2. How does Bill change his usual behavior because of his feelings for his beloved?

3. What do you think Bill learns about relationships because of this date?

4. Compare the relationship in this story with the relationship between John and Lorraine.

5. If you were Bill, would you have waited for this girl? If you were this girl, would you have wanted Bill for a boyfriend? Explain.

READING CHECK

a. How does Bill first approach his beloved?

b. How does he feel about her relationship with Sidney?

c. What problem does he face when he goes to the movies with her?

22 | The Pigman

Novel Notes

Issue 1

Introducing THE PIGMAN

Seniors a Majority?

In the last decade of the 20th century, the population of the United States grew by about 7 percent. The number of people over the age of 85, however, increased more than 30 percent. Senior citizens today are grappling with ways to remain healthy, active participants in society and family life. Clearly, senior citizens will continue to influence society through the strength of numbers.

FOR YOUR READER'S LOG

Why is this book called *The Pigman*? Is this an appropriate title? As you read the novel, look for answers to these questions, and jot notes in your Reader's Log.

NOVEL CHARACTERS MONKEY AROUND

One of the unusual characters you'll meet in *The Pigman* is a baboon. Gelada baboons are a threatened species from the high plateaus of Ethiopia. They eat roots, leaves, fruit, and the occasional insect, and can live for over 20 years. Baboon bands include up to 250 members, who find their social standing by fighting, quarreling, grooming, and chasing each other. Perhaps the oddest thing you'll see a baboon do is the "lip flip." To execute a lip flip, a baboon smiles and flips its upper lip over its nose to show off a shiny, pink mucous membrane. Scientists at first thought this was some sort of threat, but they now know that the lip flip is a friendly gesture, a calming baboon "hello."

Thinking About Thinking

History in a Nutshell

Lorraine Jensen, a character in *The Pigman*, thinks about everyone in terms of psychology—the mental and emotional reasons for behavior. Many people think psychology is a relatively new science. In fact, the ancient Greek philosopher Aristotle taught that human behavior is controlled by the soul. His study, *De anima*, written in the 4th century B.C., is considered one of the first psychological texts.

The word *psychology* also comes from ancient Greece. It is formed from the Greek root *logy*, meaning "the science or study of," and the word *psyche*, which means "breath, spirit, or soul."

Study Guide 23

Novel Notes

Issue 2

THE PIGMAN, Chapters 1–6

Get Toned Up

Tone is the attitude a writer takes toward his or her subject. With two teenagers taking turns as narrators of *The Pigman,* this novel has *two* distinct tones.

Lorraine's chapters include large words and a close look at the psychology of other characters. John's narration is distinguished by humor, sarcasm, and disguised impolite expressions. The combination of narrative styles may take some getting used to—but it certainly keeps things interesting!

FOR YOUR READER'S LOG

In your Reader's Log, make a "test" of ways to tell whether someone is showing respect for other people. As you read these chapters of *The Pigman,* decide whether John and Lorraine would pass or fail your test.

Technology Quashes Prank Calls

Lorraine and John meet the Pigman through a prank phone call. One of the reasons they make these calls is because they're pretty sure that they won't be caught.

Would they be caught today? Quite possibly. Back in the late sixties (when *The Pigman* takes place), computers didn't keep a record of every phone call. In addition, caller identification units had not yet been invented. Today people can monitor incoming phone calls to their homes and businesses. Between a customer's caller ID system and the phone company's computer tracking systems, every phone call made can now be traced.

Make Mine Mnemonic!

Angelo Pignati creates mental pictures to help him remember things. Visual images are effective mnemonic (that is, memory-helping) devices. Here are some other types of mnemonic devices:

- Key words and categorizing help learners who depend on logic.
- Imitation or pantomime will help kinesthetic learners (those who learn best through movement, like dancers or athletes).
- Many auditory learners (those who learn best through sound and music) make up rhymes and sayings that help them remember. Two of the most familiar auditory mnemonic devices are "*I* before *e* except after *c* . . ." and "Thirty days hath September, April, June, and November . . ."

Where did we get an odd word like *mnemonic*? It came from the ancient Greek goddess of memory, Mnemosyne. The Greek word for *mindful* is *mnemon;* be mindful that the first *m* is silent!

24 | *The Pigman*

Novel Notes

Issue 3

THE PIGMAN, Chapters 7–10

SALES HAVE BEAN GREAT

The Coffee Exchange, where John's father works, really exists. It has handled the buying and selling of coffee since the 1880s.

What might John do there if he took the Bore's offer? He might take phone orders from brokers who want to buy or sell large amounts of coffee, track sales times, quantities, and prices, or actually trade with other members buying and selling coffee in the "trading pit." It doesn't exactly sound like John's cup of joe, does it?

FOR YOUR READER'S LOG

How do our opinions of people change as we learn more about them? In your Reader's Log, write freely about a time when your opinion of someone changed. Compare your memories to what Lorraine and John experience in these chapters.

The Word PLACE

While many older people stay very sharp mentally, others face *senility, Alzheimer's,* or other forms of *dementia.*

Senility is a somewhat derogatory term used to describe the deterioration of the mind's functions in the elderly.

Alzheimer's disease is a specific diagnosable illness. It strikes nerve cells in the cerebral cortex, leading to physical and functional degeneration of the brain. Scientific breakthroughs have helped researchers to better understand the causes of Alzheimer's and advance their work toward a cure.

Dementia comes from a Latin term meaning "out of one's mind." It describes any number of causes for decreased intellectual power, extreme apathy, confusion, or stupor.

With research, scientists may help an aging population function well enough to decrease the need to use these terms.

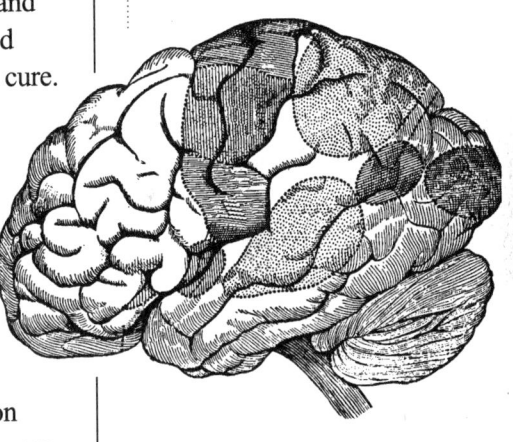

Growing through Grief

John and Lorraine must wonder why the Pigman acts as though his wife, Conchetta, is still alive when they discover evidence to the contrary in Chapter 7. Perhaps it has to do with the way that many people deal with grief.

The first stage of grief that many people experience is denial. Emerging from the numbness of denial, people often experience feelings of anger, sadness, and loneliness. Eventually, most people begin to adjust to lives without their loved ones' presence. They learn to accept the loss and go on with their lives.

Quotation Corner

"Don't be too timid and squeamish about your actions. All life is an experiment."
—Ralph Waldo Emerson

"Don't waste your time thinking about who you ought to be; just be content with who you're becoming."
—Anonymous

Study Guide | **25**

Novel Notes

Issue 4

THE PIGMAN, Chapters 11–15

Characters Can Cancel Conflicts

Like real people, the characters in *The Pigman* have to work through conflicts with each other, and, like real people, they don't always succeed. Here are five ways to help resolve those conflicts:
1. Understand your own feelings before you talk.
2. Be clear and assertive about your feelings.
3. Calmly consider the other person's point of view.
4. Express your opinion using sentences that start with "I" rather than "you," to avoid assigning blame.
5. Listen without interrupting the other person.

FOR YOUR READER'S LOG

What do you think that Lorraine and John will remember most about Mr. Pignati in the future? Make some predictions.

What's Cookin'
A TASTE OF ITALY

Angelo Pignati takes great pleasure in Italian foods. Here are some of the Italian foods Lorraine and John sample in this section of *The Pigman*.

ricotta an Italian cheese, similar in consistency to a fine curd cottage cheese
scungilli large marine snail, often cooked in a garlicky tomato sauce
spaghetti complex carbohydrate in the shape of a string; basic component of an Italian diet
vermicelli a thinner form of spaghetti

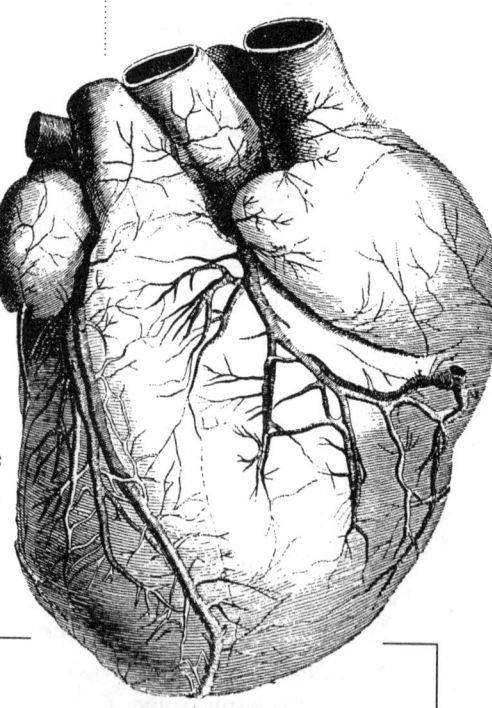

ASK the Professor

Dear Dr. I. Knoweverything,
My grandpa had a heart attack a few months ago, and he's already playing baseball with me again! Is this normal, or is my grandfather some kind of superhero?
—Pitching in Peoria

Dear Pitching,
Your grandfather may be a superhero, but his recovery is fairly normal. Most heart attack survivors can resume normal activities within two months.

So what is a heart attack? It's when heart muscle cells die because their blood supply has been cut off, usually by a blood clot or cholesterol buildup. This cell death can interfere with signals that tell the heart to beat, which in turn can lead to death. Over 90% of heart attack patients who make it to the hospital survive, though, and administering CPR as soon as possible saves many lives. Doctors can also inflate a small balloon inside the clogged artery to open up blood flow. The hospital staff monitors a patient for three to six days, gradually increasing the patient's activity level until he or she is ready to go home.

To prevent another heart attack, doctors can prescribe medications, and patients can stop smoking, lose weight, improve their diets, and exercise, as your grandfather is doing. Play ball!

26 | *The Pigman*

Novel Notes

Issue 5

THE PIGMAN, Connections

Writers Do Read Letters Written by Readers

After finishing an enjoyable book, many readers want to share their responses with the author. Here are some ways to get in touch with a favorite author:

- To use e-mail, do an Internet search using the name of the author or the name of the company that published the book. Or follow links from the Internet Public Library Web site at http://www.ipl.org/youth/AskAuthor/ to reach a writer's home page.
- Two frequently updated books by Michael Levine are excellent resources for author addresses—*The Address Book: How to Reach Anyone Who Is Anyone* and *The Kid's Address Book: Over 3,000 Addresses of Celebrities, Athletes, Entertainers, and More*. Librarians can help you find other sources in addition to these.
- The publisher's mailing address can be found on the back of the book's title page. Publishers will forward letters to the author.

Connections

- A Personal Note
- Happy Birthday
- My First Love

FOR YOUR READER'S LOG

In your Reader's Log, write a motto or slogan that could help people face the challenges of growing up well and learn from them. Think about your motto or slogan as you read the Connections.

They Beat the Summer Birthday Blues

Like Ollie in "Happy Birthday," these people missed out on having their lockers decorated on their birthdays. Still, they seem to have turned out just fine.

June 14: Laurence Yep, author
July 4: Louis Armstrong, musician; Ann Landers and Abigail Van Buren, advice columnists
July 7: Lisa Leslie, basketball star
July 31: Richard Rodriguez, journalist and author
Aug. 5: Neil Armstrong, test pilot and astronaut
Aug. 12: Walter Dean Myers, fiction writer and poet.

By the way, Toni Cade Bambara, the author of "Happy Birthday," didn't share Ollie's problem—she was born on March 25th.

History in a Nutshell

Love Letters Nothing New

Abelard and Heloise may be history's most famous passers of love notes. Here's a sample from Abelard's pen:

"Under the pretext of study we spent our hours in the happiness of love.... Our speech was more of love than of the books which lay open before us."

Their legendary love survived the objections of Heloise's family, and their letters have survived from the twelfth century. After they were secretly married, a tragedy forced them apart. Heloise became an abbess and Abelard a monk—but their letters continued. They are buried together in Paris.

Study Guide 27

Novel Notes

Issue 6

THE PIGMAN, Connections

Writers Paint Vivid Pictures

Photographers and artists capture images using tools such as film and paint. Writers can use words in the same way, as tools to communicate images to their readers.

In "Fifth Grade Autobiography," Rita Dove creates a powerful image in the reader's mind based on an old photograph of her grandfather.

Margarita Mondrus Engle, author of "Niña," turns this idea on its head, leading her readers to develop mental images of the photos her narrator *didn't* take. Either way, words can rival film in creating memorable pictures.

Connections

- Abuela Invents the Zero
- Fifth Grade Autobiograhy
- Abuela
- Lineage
- Niña

Lend a Hand

WANTED Teenagers to help out in the community through volunteer service. Opportunities include visiting the elderly, teaching sports or crafts to children, working to improve the environment, helping the homeless or people with long-term illnesses, caring for animals, working for equal rights for all, and enhancing our cultural community. There's something for everyone!

If community service interests you, find out about volunteer programs through your school and the yellow pages. Remember, by helping others, you help yourself!

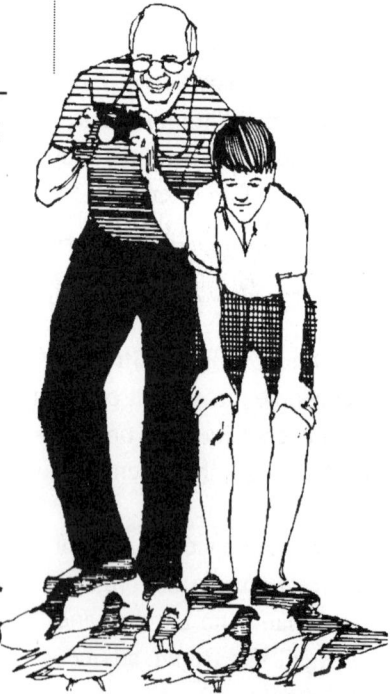

Life Expectancy Rises

As old as Mr. Pignati seems to Lorraine and John, he would be positively Paleolithic to people in ancient Greece, when the average person lived only 28 years. Even during the 20th century, life spans increased dramatically, as the following graph shows.

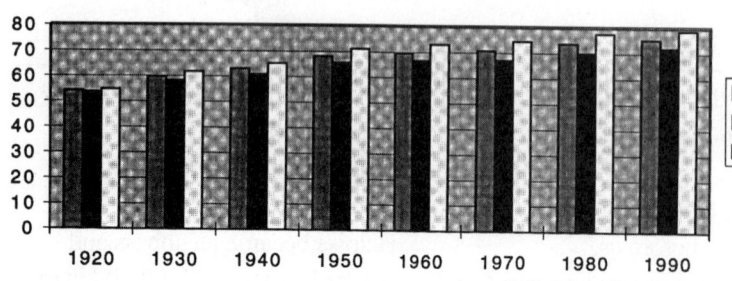

20th-Century Life Spans

For Your Reader's Log

If you could live a long life, how would you want to be remembered at its end? Jot down a few ideas in your Reader's Log. As you read the Connections, see if your ideas change.

The Pigman

Name _____

Reading Skills and Strategies Worksheet

Novel Organizer — *The Pigman*

CHARACTER

Use the chart below to keep track of the characters in this book. Each time you come across a new character, write the character's name and the number of the page on which the character first appears. Then, jot down a brief description. Add information about the characters as you read. Put a star next to the name of each main character.

NAME OF CHARACTER	PAGE	DESCRIPTION

Study Guide | 29

Name _____

Reading Skills and Strategies Worksheet

Novel Organizer *(continued)* — *The Pigman*

SETTING

Where and when does this story take place? ....

CONFLICT (Read at least one chapter before you answer.)

What is the biggest problem faced by the main character(s)? ....

How do you predict it will be resolved? ....

MAJOR EVENTS

-
-
-
-
-

OUTCOME

How is the main problem resolved? (How accurate was your prediction?) ....

30 | *The Pigman*

Name _____ Date _____

Reading Skills and Strategies Worksheet
The Pigman

Chapters 1–6: Noting Settings

Setting is the time and place in which events happen. Everything in *The Pigman* happens on Staten Island in the late sixties. Within that large setting, though, there are several smaller settings.

Briefly describe each setting below, and explain why it is important to the story.

1. *Setting:* John's house

    Description: ....

    Importance: ....

    ....

    ....

2. *Setting:* Mr. Pignati's house

    Description: ....

    Importance: ....

    ....

    ....

3. *Setting:* Lorraine's house

    Description: ....

    Importance: ....

    ....

    ....

4. *Setting:* the Primate Building at the Baron Park Zoo

    Description: ....

    Importance: ....

    ....

    ....

Name _____ Date _____

Reading Skills and Strategies Worksheet
The Pigman

Chapters 7–10: Responding to Quotations

In the left-hand column, write down several quotations from this part of the novel that catch your attention. **In the right-hand column, jot down a response to each quotation.** You might ask a question about it, describe how it makes you feel, or connect it to other stories that you have read.

QUOTATION	RESPONSE

32 | *The Pigman*

Name _____ Date _____

Reading Skills and Strategies Worksheet
The Pigman

Chapters 11–15: Identifying Consequences

Consider the choices that the characters in *The Pigman* have made, as well as the consequences of those choices.

In the chart below, write the consequences of each choice listed.

CHOICE	CONSEQUENCE
At the hospital, Mr. Pignati tells Lorraine and John to keep his house keys.	
John and Lorraine dress up in clothes they find at the Pigman's house.	
John and Lorraine host a party at the Pigman's house.	
John calls Mr. Pignati to apologize.	
Mr. Pignati accepts their invitation to visit the zoo again.	

Study Guide | **33**

Name _____   Date _____

Literary Elements Worksheet

The Pigman

Point of View

Because this story is told by two first-person narrators, readers see the events through two different points of view.

In the space provided, write the name of the narrator whose point of view is expressed in each of the following statements.

1. "When I look at Miss Reillen I feel sorry. When I hear her walking I feel even more sorry for her because maybe she keeps her mother in a bed in the middle of the living room just like Miss Stewart." ....

2. "The only thing I do now that is faintly criminal is write on desks. Like right this minute I feel like writing something on the nice polished table here, and since the Cricket is down at the other end of the library showing some four-eyed dimwit how to use the encyclopedias, I'm going to do it." ....

3. "He could've been some psycho with an electric carving knife who'd dismember our bodies and wouldn't get caught until our teeth clogged up the sewer or something like that." ....

4. "There was enough artillery in Beekman's toy department to wipe out Red China and the Mau-Mau tribe of Africa, and I personally think some of the toy manufacturers could use a good course in preventative psychiatry." ....

5. "We really went to work on the house and fixed it up better than ever before. The only room we didn't touch was the one with the pigs in it. There was something almost religious about that room, as though it contained a spirit that belonged only to Mr. Pignati, and it was best left alone." ....

6. "Maybe I would rather be dead than to turn into the kind of grown-up people I knew. What was so hot about living anyway if people think you're a disturbing influence just because you still think about God and Death and the Universe and Love." ....

Briefly explain how you can tell the difference between Lorraine's point of view and John's.

....
....
....
....

Name _____ Date _____

Literary Elements Worksheet

The Pigman

Foreshadowing

Foreshadowing is the use of hints or clues to suggest events that will occur later in a story. Explore the foreshadowing in *The Pigman* by completing this chart. **Next to each event in the column on the left, write the related event that is foreshadowed.** (Hint: Sometimes a later event is foreshadowed by more than one detail.)

EARLIER EVENT	LATER EVENT
1. Lorraine admits that John is compassionate, even though it doesn't seem that way on the surface.	
2. The tour of the Pignati house focuses on the pig collection.	
3. Lorraine wonders about couples who die within a short time of each other.	
4. At Chambers Street, Lorraine sees a woman who repeats, "Death is coming."	
5. Norton threatens to steal electronics from the Pignati house.	
6. Mr. Pignati says that Bobo refused to eat his chocolate bar and is getting old.	
7. Lorraine dreams of a coffin in the pig room.	

Study Guide **35**

Glossary

The Pigman

- Words are listed by chapter in their order of appearance.
- The definition and the part of speech are based on the way the word is used in the chapter. For other uses of the word, check a dictionary.
- **Vocabulary Words** are preceded by an asterisk (*) and appear in the Vocabulary Worksheet.

Chapter 1

*avocation *n.*: work or hobby done in addition to regular work

*excruciatingly *adv.*: intensely, to the point of being painful

Chapter 2

*subliminally *adv.*: below the level of awareness

thrombosis *n.*: formation of blood clot in a blood vessel, which can produce a heart attack

*compassion *n.*: ability to sympathize with and try to ease another's distress

*compulsive *adj.*: uncontrollable

paranoia *n.*: mental illness marked by feelings of persecution and distrust

*mortified *adj.*: extremely embarrassed

Chapter 4

*philanthropy *n.*: generosity toward others that attempts to improve their way of life

*prevaricates *v.*: tells a lie

Chapter 5

hypertension *n.*: high blood pressure

*subconscious *n.*: mental activity just below consciousness

*dismember *v.*: cut up into pieces

Chapter 6

*antagonistic *adj.*: opposing; disagreeable

*nocturnal *adj.*: active at night

Chapter 7

voluptuous *adj.*: richly beautiful; shapely but slightly plump

*floundering *v.*: struggling without success

*ingrate *n.*: ungrateful person

Chapter 8

*delicacies *n.*: delicious, fancy foods; gourmet foods

Chapter 9

berserk *adj.*: crazily reckless

Chapter 10

*fixated *adj.*: obsessively focused on something

*muttered *v.*: said in a soft, mumbling voice

Chapter 11

*graft *n.*: money earned illegally, especially by overlooking someone's wrongdoing

bubonic plague *n.*: contagious bacterial disease

Chapter 12

maladjusted *v.*: poorly adjusted

*hovel *n.*: small, miserable house

Chapter 13

*bellowed *v.*: shouted in a loud voice

Chapter 14

*incongruous *adj.*: mismatched; inconsistent

*disheartened *adj.*: depressed; without hope

pathetic *adj.*: causing pity or deep sadness

Chapter 15

trespassing *n.*: intruding; wrongfully entering someone else's property

Name _____ Date _____

Vocabulary Worksheet

The Pigman

A. Match each word in the left-hand column with the correct meaning from the right-hand column. Write the letter of the definition in the space provided.

_____ 1. antagonistic   a. mumbled

_____ 2. graft   b. with painful intensity

_____ 3. delicacies   c. not matching

_____ 4. muttered   d. uncontrollable

_____ 5. avocation   e. struggling but failing

_____ 6. hovel   f. a small, miserable house

_____ 7. excruciatingly   g. illegal payment

_____ 8. compulsive   h. cut up

_____ 9. incongruous   i. gourmet foods

_____ 10. philanthropy   j. opposing

_____ 11. floundering   k. charity

_____ 12. dismember   l. hobby

B. In an *analogy,* pairs of words are related in the same way. In the space provided, complete each of the following analogies with a word from the box. (You will not use every word.)

| nocturnal | subliminally | fixated | prevaricates | bellowed |
| compassion | subliminally disheartened | fixated subconscious | prevaricates mortified | bellowed ingrate |

13. _____ : cry :: encouraged : smile

14. sympathy : _____ :: fondness : affection

15. eyes : riveted :: mind : _____

16. _____ : darkness :: aquatic : water

17. stomped : feet :: _____ : voice

18. thankfulness : _____ :: wisdom : fool

19. promising : pledges :: lying : _____

20. embarrass : _____ :: praise : proud

Study Guide | 37

Name _____ Date _____

TEST   PART I: OBJECTIVE QUESTIONS

Identify the character that best completes each statement about *The Pigman*. (12 points)

_____ 1. _____ hopes to become an actor someday.

_____ 2. Being a famous writer is the goal of _____.

_____ 3. The memory game is presented by _____.

_____ 4. As a nurse, _____ works long hours and weekends.

_____ 5. *The Bore* is a nickname for _____.

_____ 6. At the zoo, Angelo Pignati likes to feed peanuts to _____.

In the spaces provided, mark each true statement *T* and each false statement *F*. (18 points)

_____ 7. John and Lorraine make prank telephone calls.

_____ 8. Lorraine and John meet the Pigman because of a school project.

_____ 9. Mr. Pignati's wife is on a trip in California.

_____ 10. John's father offers him a job.

_____ 11. Lorraine and John pretend they are Mr. Pignati's children.

_____ 12. Lorraine's mother shows respect for her patients.

_____ 13. John suggests that he and Lorraine host a party at the Pigman's house.

_____ 14. John gets drunk and destroys the pig collection.

_____ 15. The Pigman cries when he finds out that his favorite animal has died.

The Pigman

Name _____ Date _____

TEST — PART II: SHORT-ANSWER QUESTIONS

Answer each question, using the lines provided. *(40 points)*

16. Why do John and Lorraine so often find themselves in trouble?

17. Why do Lorraine and John end up at the zoo?

18. Whose thoughts and feelings about the events in the novel does the reader experience? How do you know?

19. How would you describe John's relationship with his family?

20. How would you describe life in Lorraine's home?

Study Guide | 39

TEST — PART II: SHORT-ANSWER QUESTIONS (continued)

21. How do John and Lorraine agree and disagree in their feelings about school?

22. What truths do Lorraine, John, and Mr. Pignati share about themselves after the day at Beekman's Department Store?

23. What purpose does Norton Kelly play in this novel?

24. What does Angelo Pignati find when he returns home from the hospital?

25. What factors contribute to the death of the Pigman?

Name _____ Date _____

TEST — PART III: ESSAY QUESTIONS

Choose *two* of the following topics. Use your own paper to write two or three paragraphs about each topic you choose. *(30 points)*

a. Do Lorraine and John have a good friendship? What do they have in common? Do their differences help or harm their friendship? Write an explanation of the friendship, giving examples from the novel to support your ideas.

b. Do you consider John and Lorraine murderers? Imagine that you are on a jury, and explain your judgment of the behavior of John and Lorraine and their role in Mr. Pignati's death.

c. Imagine that six months have passed since Mr. Pignati has died. As Lorraine and John think about their experiences with him, what have they learned? Write a diary entry, either for Lorraine or for John, telling what the experiences of *The Pigman* have taught her or him.

d. John and Lorraine respect each other, and they learn to respect Mr. Pignati. However, they do not respect their parents, most of their teachers and school officials, and many of their classmates. Explain what you think *respect* means to Lorraine and John. Then tell whether you think that definition is accurate—and why.

e. John says that if "we hadn't come along the Pigman would've just lived like a vegetable until he died alone in that dump of a house." Try turning that idea around. What do you think would have happened to John and Lorraine if the Pigman hadn't come along? Explain your answer.

Use this space to make notes.

Study Guide | 41

Answer Key

The Pigman

Chapters 1–6: Making Meanings

> **READING CHECK**
> a. The Bathroom Bomber is John, who has set off firecracker bombs in a school bathroom.
> b. The Cricket is Miss Reillen, the librarian, whose nylon stockings rub together and make a chirping sound.
> c. The Marshmallow Kid is Norton, who was once caught shoplifting marshmallows.
> d. The Bore is John's father; the term expresses John's interpretation of his father's life and character.
> e. The Pigman is Angelo Pignati; Mr. and Mrs. Pignati gathered a large collection of pig figurines during their marriage.

1. Answers will vary. Some students may suggest that Lorraine, who has more compassion, would be a better friend than John; Some might consider John more fun to be with; other students may find both characters too different from themselves to make likely friends.

2. John says in Chapter 3, "Lorraine remembers the big words, and I remember the action." John's writing is more emotional and blunt, and it has a sarcastic or even bitter tone. Lorraine's style is more analytical and objective in approach and tone, but she seems to have more sympathy for her subjects.

3. John may want to do outlandish things to prove that he will never become a bore like his father. In addition, he earns respect from his peers when he performs a prank successfully.

4. Lorraine is no "true-man"; she is far from telling the truth about herself and the reason for contacting Mr. Pignati. In addition, she frequently lies to her mother about where she spends her time. John seems to be a "wanderer," looking for a way to fit in or make his mark on the world as he approaches adulthood.

5. Pignati seems to have a naturally generous spirit. He also is desperately lonely because of his wife's recent death. His generosity may be a means of securing his visitors' friendship.

6. They probably enjoy the release of emotions as they howl together. In this scene, we see that John and Lorraine are forming a bond with Mr. Pignati—that despite their age difference, they have something in common.

7. Answers will vary. Some students might want to confront John's rebelliousness, to explore Lorraine's interest in psychology, or to find out more about Pignati's personal history, for example.

8. Answers will vary. Based on differing life experiences, some students may feel dishonesty is never justified, while others may list reasons why people sometimes lie.

9. Some students may feel strongly that they would not have revealed Pignati's death. A few students may suggest that knowing this fact so early makes them look at the story in a different and more interesting way.

Chapters 7–10: Making Meanings

> **READING CHECK**
> John's chapters include a trip to the cemetery; dinner at his house; a visit to Mr. Pignati's house, where he finds the funeral bill for Mrs. Pignati; and a meeting with Norton, who threatens to steal the Pigman's electronics. Lorraine's chapters include the visit to Beekman's Department Store, the revelation of truths at Pignati's home, and the roller-skating game that ends with Pignati's heart attack.

1. Answers will vary. Students may have felt happiest during the adventure at Beekman's, saddest at the Conlans' dinner conversation or Mr. Pignati's tears over his late wife, and surprised by the purchase of the roller skates or by Pignati's heart attack.

(cont.)

Answer Key (continued)

The Pigman

2. Some students will say that the scene confirms John's opinion of his parents, for the conversation seems to suggest that they don't understand him at all. A few students, however, may notice that some details (such as Mr. Conlan's "I want you to be your own man" and Mrs. Conlan's concern for her husband's health) suggest that these two are not merely one-dimensional characters.

3. Students may find evidence of the power of love in the way that Pignati has been left so lonely by the death of his beloved Conchetta. They also may see it in the way that Lorraine and John begin to soften because of their contact with him.

4. As the scene opens, the atmosphere is tense because the Pigman seems so weak and low. The atmosphere turns very sad when the characters all tell the truth and Mr. Pignati starts to cry because he misses Conchetta. The mood becomes happier as everyone plays the psychological game and becomes exciting and fun as they roller-skate through the house. Suddenly, though, the mood turns frightening and grim when Mr. Pignati has a heart attack and collapses on the stairs.

5. John has lost his characteristic sarcasm when it comes to Mr. Pignati. He vows to kill Norton if Norton should ever hurt the older man. When Pignati weeps over Conchetta, John sympathizes with a tenderness that surprises even Lorraine.

6. Answers will be personal and need not be shared. Encourage students to think about specific actions that lead them to their comparisons.

7. Students may suggest that a married couple might share such a strong bond that when one person dies, the other loses the will to live. Some students may suggest that Lorraine's comment here indicates that this will be the case with the Pignatis, as well.

8. Some students may find the many "real-life" writings distracting; other students may feel that they help hold the readers' interest by allowing them to "see" through Lorraine and John's eyes. Students may suggest that including such details helps make the story seem more true to life.

Chapters 11–15: Making Meanings

> **READING CHECK**
> Major details and events include Lorraine and John's private, romantic dinner; the difficulties that both characters have with their parents; the breakfast and argument at Mr. Pignati's; the disastrous party and the Pigman's return; John and Lorraine's phone call to Mr. Pignati; and the final visit to the zoo, during which Mr. Pignati dies.

1. Answers will vary, but most students will express sadness over Mr. Pignati's death. A few students may comment upon what John and Lorraine may have learned through knowing him.

2. They argue because they are uncomfortable with the change in their relationship.

3. The party increases the tension of the story; readers feel that this disaster will push the action closer to some sort of climax. It also increases the conflict among the main characters; readers wonder how the Pigman will react to the discovery of what his friends have done.

4. He still likes Lorraine and John and wants to spend time with them. At the same time, he is deeply hurt by their betrayal of his trust—especially because their party has led to the destruction of possessions that were dear to him and Conchetta.

5. Students should note that Bobo was very special to Mr. Pignati. Because the Pignatis loved to visit the zoo, perhaps Bobo represented the enjoyment that Angelo Pignati took from doing

(cont.)

Answer Key (continued)

The Pigman

things with Conchetta. Perhaps he feels that Bobo is, in a sense, his child. Students also may suggest that by being in a cage, Bobo symbolizes Mr. Pignati's feeling of being trapped in a life of loneliness.

6. Among the lessons students may cite are the following: People tend to focus their lives on unimportant things; they are becoming adults, with the power to influence other people's lives and to control their own destinies; they too will face old age and death someday; rules make life easier but less meaningful; our society treats the elderly badly.

7. Some students may comment that the best thing to have done would be to "pull the plug" and make everyone leave—or to leave on their own and hope that others would follow their example.

8. Answers will vary. Encourage students to offer specific suggestions about taking an interest in older or younger people's lives and showing appreciation for their abilities and achievements.

9. Many students will wish that Mr. Pignati had not died and may feel that John and Lorraine already had learned a great lesson about compassion and respect for other people. Other students may feel that Pignati's death drives home the idea that a person should be compassionate and respectful while life offers the opportunity to do so, as well as the fact that their own lives will have an ending and that they have the power to live in a meaningful way before that ending comes.

Exploring the Connections

A Personal Note: Making Meanings

READING CHECK
a. A fifteen-year-old boy trespassed on Zindel's property. The boy had some of the characteristics and problems that Zindel later built into John Conlan.
b. The teenage boy that Zindel met had a girlfriend who cried every time someone mentioned war because she knew someone who had been shot and killed.
c. Zindel used memories of his own mother, who had both a difficult and a nice side in real life.
d. Zindel used memories of trouble that he himself caused as a teenager.
e. Zindel tried to imagine what a person who collected pigs would be like because he had heard, from a friend over dinner, about a man who collected piggy banks.

1. Answers will vary, but many students will feel that Zindel sounds very much like someone from the world of the novel.

2. According to Zindel, an "honest novel" is like a dream in that both contain people who are "extension[s] of your emotional self."

3. Answers will vary, but students may suggest that his comments confirm their suspicion that there is more to the parents than we might see in the novel.

4. He probably would encourage writers to write from the heart and to be honest in what they say. He might urge them not to worry about spelling and other technical matters until they have drafted their ideas.

5. Answers will vary. Encourage students to list questions they would ask about characters and plot details, or suggestions of ideas for books they would like to see him write.

(cont.)

Answer Key (continued) — The Pigman

Happy Birthday: Making Meanings

READING CHECK
a. The story is set in an urban neighborhood during the summertime.
b. Ollie Larkins is an orphaned girl who lives with her grandfather. Her problem is that no one seems to know that it is her birthday.

1. At first, Ollie just seems to be an ill-tempered critic; it is hard to feel for her. When we realize why she is out of sorts, and as we watch her soften to the point of tears, we come to care more about her.

2. *Happy birthday* are the words that Ollie desperately wants to hear, but no one says them. This birthday turns out to be an unhappy day for her.

3. The story uses a third-person point of view that seems to be omniscient. Students may suggest that the story would have been more personal—perhaps too painfully so—if Ollie had told it herself.

4. Students may suggest that both stories are realistic, set in urban neighborhoods; that their characters are young people, many of whom tend to get in trouble; and that the stories show both the humor and sadness in the lives of kids.

5. Answers will vary and may reflect students' feelings about their own birthdays. Students may feel that some people like being the center of attention or enjoy feeling special on their birthday, while others prefer not to be singled out or do not observe birthdays for religious reasons.

Abuela Invents the Zero
Making Meanings

READING CHECK
a. According to Connie, the visit was "so that she wouldn't die without seeing snow."
b. Connie doesn't want the people who know her to know that she is related to someone who looks so ridiculous and acts oddly.
c. When Abuela needed Connie's help, Connie did nothing. She made Abuela "feel like a zero, like a nothing."

1. While students may understand Connie's embarrassment and remorse, many students may feel more sympathy for Abuela, who is deeply saddened by Connie's apparent lack of concern.

2. Students may describe Connie as *self-centered, worried about appearances,* and perhaps, *able to learn from experience.* Abuela could be described as *old-fashioned, sad,* and *looking for affection.*

3. Connie feels very awkward about the differences between her generation and Abuela's. As a result, she causes Abuela to redefine *zero* in human terms—to mean "a person who has no importance." Like Lorraine and John, Connie realizes that she was wrong about Abuela after the older woman has shared her feelings.

4. Students may suggest that for most of the story, Connie sounds like John; both freely criticize the people and situations around them. Toward the end of the story, Connie's realization of her grandmother's feelings may sound a little more like Lorraine.

Answer Key (continued)

The Pigman

5. Many students might wish to have the story go on to show a reconciliation between Connie and Abuela. Some students may suggest that leaving matters unresolved shows that it is not always easy to repair our mistakes or that leaving Connie deep in thought makes the reader think more about his or her own relationships.

Fifth Grade Autobiography / Abuela / Lineage: Making Meanings

> **READING CHECK**
>
> Answers may resemble the following:
>
> *for "Fifth Grade Autobiography":* Although time passes, strong memories stay in your heart.
>
> *for "Abuela":* My grandmother's lively spirit will be missed when she is gone.
>
> *for "Lineage":* I wish I had the strength that my grandmothers had.

1. Answers will vary, but students should support their answers with details and perhaps quotations from the poem they choose.
2. Qualities include loving hearts, stability, the need to pass down family lore, and physical and emotional strength.
3. For the most part, "Fifth Grade Autobiography" takes an objective or just slightly nostalgic tone; "Abuela" is warm and conversational; and "Lineage" is praising and wistful.
4. Answers will be personal and need not be shared. Encourage students to think about specific comparisons.
5. Many students may feel that the poems remind them of Lorraine, who writes more from the heart than John does.

Niña: Making Meanings

> **READING CHECK**
>
> a. They are told not to tell anyone that they are tomboys, not to brag about how much money they have, and not to bring animals into the house. She disobeys all of them.
>
> b. All we know is that "she has a hole in her stomach." Whatever the problem is, it results in Niña's death.

1. Most students will feel sad for Niña, whose family could not afford the medical help that might have saved her life. They may feel some resentment for the narrator's lack of compassion but appreciate the fact that she has come to recognize her short-sightedness.
2. The narrator may not care what the people in Cuba think, or she may want them to be jealous of her. On the other hand, she may just be speaking without thinking. She may also gain a sense of power from disobeying her mother's instructions.
3. The narrator of "Niña" is like Lorraine and John in the early part of the novel because she does not consider the wishes and problems of others. For example, the narrator doesn't think about the fact that Niña will die because she is poor and sick, and John and Lorraine do not consider how sick Mr. Pignati is when they take advantage of their relationship with him.
4. Students may suggest a moral relating to the importance of treating other people as individuals or to the need to be sensitive to another's weakness.
5. Answers will vary, but many students may cite events and details from the story to suggest that the American cousin would be seen as proud and self-centered.

(cont.)

Answer Key (continued)

The Pigman

My First Love: Making Meanings

> **READING CHECK**
>
> a. He passes a note to her "constant girlfriend" and starts a correspondence with her.
>
> b. He is willing to "get in line" to be the girl's boyfriend, sure that he is cuter than Sidney and eventually will replace him.
>
> c. He has to go to the bathroom but finds it hard to move because his arm has fallen asleep. He is afraid his date will think less of him if he admits either problem.

1. Most students will find the story funny, both because of its basic situation and because Cosby is willing to poke fun at himself.

2. He becomes obsessive about being clean and well groomed; he finds himself at a loss for words; he waits patiently for the girl to break up with two boyfriends before getting around to him.

3. Students may conclude that he learned to feel more comfortable with himself or that he learned not to worry about how he thought he should act to impress others.

4. Students may note that the relationships are similar in that there were awkward moments and shyness in both, but that they differ because Lorraine and John knew each other well before becoming romantically involved and their relationship seems likely to last longer because of their shared experiences.

5. Answers will vary. Some students may feel that the girl doesn't seem interested enough in Bill to make her worth the wait, but that Bill is enthusiastic and funny enough to make him a good choice for a boyfriend.

Reading Skills and Strategies Worksheets

Chapters 1–6: Noting Settings

Answers may resemble the following:

1. *Setting:* John's house

   Description: almost painfully, obsessively clean; not a welcoming place

   Importance: Because of the emotional coldness of this setting, John stays away as often as he can. Staying away from home often means getting into trouble, which is how he meets the Pigman.

2. *Setting:* Mr. Pignati's house

   Description: "a phenomenal dump," with old, cheap furniture, a lot of clutter, and a room full of pig figurines

   Importance: It is here that John and Lorraine first get to know Mr. Pignati. They form a bond that makes his home seem a nicer place to be than their own homes.

3. *Setting:* Lorraine's house

   Description: not very well kept; a place full of her mother's complaints

   Importance: Like John, Lorraine doesn't like being at home. She, too, tries to get away as often as she can.

4. *Setting:* the Primate Building at the Baron Park Zoo

   Description: filled with barred cages; smelly and noisy

   Importance: Bobo the baboon lives here, so it is the Pigman's favorite place to visit. In Chapter 6, Lorraine, John, and the Pigman let off steam and become better friends when they howl like monkeys in the Primate Building.

(cont.)

Answer Key (continued)

The Pigman

Chapters 7–10: Responding to Quotations

Quotations will vary. One possible quotation and response for each of the three main characters follows.

Quotation	Response
"I think cemeteries are one of the loveliest places to be—if you're not dead, of course. The hills and green grass and flowers are much nicer than what you get when you're alive."	Most cemeteries are well kept, but it seems creepy to spend time in one. Everybody is curious about dying, I guess. I wonder if John will find the answers he wants.
"[I]f I didn't wear the roller skates, I'd be letting him down. I'd be disappointing him in the main thing that he liked about me."	Roller-skating through a department store sounds like fun! I think that Lorraine cares about John much more deeply than she realizes right now.
"We loved each other. We didn't need anyone else. She did everything for me. We were each other's life."	Poor Mr. Pignati—I feel so sad for him! Watching him makes me have more sympathy for the older single people I know.

Chapters 11–15: Identifying Consequences

See the following for a suggested chart.

CHOICE	CONSEQUENCE
At the hospital, Mr. Pignati tells Lorraine and John to keep his house keys.	They use the house to pretend to be adults, sharing a romantic dinner and hosting a destructive party.
John and Lorraine dress up in clothes they find at the Pigman's house.	Each finds the other more attractive, and they kiss.
John and Lorraine host a party at the Pigman's house.	The party is a disaster, resulting in damage to the pig collection and in a run-in with the police.
John calls Mr. Pignati to apologize.	Their friendship is restored.
Mr. Pignati accepts their invitation to visit the zoo again.	When he hears that Bobo has died, Mr. Pignati collapses and dies, too.

Literary Elements Worksheets

Point of View

1. Lorraine
2. John
3. John
4. Lorraine
5. Lorraine
6. John

In general, John speaks his mind, even if he is blunt, shocking, or mean-spirited. He tends to present his thoughts in terms of the daring or the sensational. Lorraine analyzes and finds reasons. She tends to present her thoughts in a more intellectual way, with compassion and with a sense of the spiritual aspects of life.

Answer Key (continued)

The Pigman

Foreshadowing

Descriptions of later events may resemble the following.

EARLIER EVENT	LATER EVENT
1. Lorraine admits that John is compassionate, even though it doesn't seem that way on the surface.	John expresses compassion for Mr. Pignati when the older man cries for his late wife. When the Pigman dies, John shows compassion by staying by his side.
2. The tour of the Pignati house focuses on the pig collection.	Much of the pig collection, which means a great deal to Mr. Pignati, is destroyed by Norton during the party.
3. Lorraine wonders about couples who die within a short time of each other.	Conchetta Pignati has died about a month before Lorraine and John meet the Pigman, and he dies a few months later.
4. At Chambers Street, Lorraine sees a woman who repeats, "Death is coming."	The woman's words are an omen, pointing to Mr. Pignati's death at the novel's end.
5. Norton threatens to steal electronics from the Pignati house.	Norton becomes a force that creates problems for John and Lorraine and their relationship with Mr. Pignati.
6. Mr. Pignati says that Bobo refused to eat his chocolate bar and is getting old.	Bobo dies of pneumonia.
7. Lorraine dreams of a coffin in the pig room.	Many of the pigs are destroyed and this shock may slow Mr. Pignati's recovery; he dies.

Vocabulary Worksheet

If you wish to score this worksheet, assign the point values given in parentheses.

A. *(5 points each)*

1. j
2. g
3. i
4. a
5. l
6. f
7. b
8. d
9. c
10. k
11. e
12. h

B. *(5 points each)*

13. disheartened
14. compassion
15. fixated
16. nocturnal
17. bellowed
18. ingrate
19. prevaricates
20. mortified

Test

Part I: Objective Questions

1. John (John Conlan)
2. Lorraine (Lorraine Jensen)
3. the Pigman (Mr. Pignati; Angelo Pignati)
4. Mrs. Jensen (Lorraine's mother)
5. Mr. Conlan (John's father)
6. Bobo (the baboon)

Study Guide | 49

Answer Key (continued)

The Pigman

7. T
8. F
9. F
10. T
11. T
12. F
13. T
14. F
15. F

Part II: Short-Answer Questions

16. Both Lorraine and John avoid their unpleasant homes as much as possible, and neither fits in well with other students. Looking for things to do outside of family and school often lands them in trouble—especially with the school and parents they are trying to avoid.

17. After a prank phone call, John and Lorraine go to Mr. Pignati's house to collect a donation, pretending that they are charity workers. They accept his invitation to visit the zoo with him.

18. Lorraine and John share their thoughts and feelings. They both use the pronoun *I* to identify themselves, and each comments upon the other's narration.

19. John considers his family—his parents and his older brother—boring, unimaginative, and unaware of his interests, hopes, and dreams.

20. Lorraine's home life is unpleasant. Her mother is demanding, unhappy, and suspicious. The house itself is untidy and there is little money for even the basic necessities.

21. They both are critical of teachers and other school personnel, but Lorraine shows that she tries to understand at least some of them. They both cut classes when they feel that they have something better to do, but Lorraine takes her studies more seriously.

22. Lorraine and John confess that they are not charity workers, and Mr. Pignati confesses that his wife is dead.

23. Norton Kelly is a troublemaker who foreshadows the trouble that John and Lorraine will have later at their party. He creates suspense in any scene in which he appears.

24. When Mr. Pignati arrives home from the hospital, he finds a party where kids are drinking, music is being played loudly, and his belongings have been trashed.

25. Mr. Pignati's fatal heart attack may have been triggered by the shock of Bobo's death and by John and Lorraine's betrayal of his trust while he was still recovering from the first heart attack. His loneliness and grief may have also contributed to his poor health.

Part III: Essay Questions

Students should respond to two out of the five essay topics. Answers will vary but should include specific references to the text.

a. They are good friends because in certain ways they are opposites and their personalities complement each other. A similarity between them is the distance they feel from their families, which encourages them to depend on each other. As opposites, John likes to act boldly (roller skating through Beekman's and having a party at the Pigman's house, for example), which brings Lorraine out of her shell. Lorraine sets an example of compassion toward others for John, softening his rough edges, and helps John understand his behavior by explaining it in terms of psychology.

b. Most students would not consider John and Lorraine to be murderers. Some students may feel (as Lorraine seems to feel) that John and Lorraine's actions caused the stress that brought on Mr. Pignati's heart attack. On the other hand, the heart attack may have resulted from natural

Answer Key (continued) — *The Pigman*

causes that did not involve Lorraine and John at all. One even could argue that by giving Pignati a purpose in his existence, they prolonged his life.

c. Students' entries should reflect a sense of perspective following the character's initial grief. The character may express a greater understanding of other people and mention personal relationships that have improved as a result. The character also may express gratitude for having known Angelo Pignati.

d. Students may suggest that to John and Lorraine, *respect* involves both looking up to and looking after people who show concern for them and interest in their ideas. Students may feel that that definition is rather self-centered and that respect can be earned by a person because of his or her inner strengths—not just because of what he or she can do to support another person. Students may also agree with Lorraine and John that people in positions of authority do not automatically deserve their respect, but must earn it through their actions.

e. Answers will vary. John may have gotten into more and more trouble until he wound up in jail; Lorraine may have isolated herself more from life. Students should demonstrate an understanding that Mr. Pignati's influence helped both Lorraine and John to become more accepting of others and more responsible for their own actions.

Notes

Notes

Notes